GROUNDBREAKERS

Christopher Columbus

Struan Reid

Heinemann

H **www.heinemann.co.uk/library**
Visit our website to find out more information about **Heinemann Library** books.

To order:
☎ Phone 44 (0) 1865 888066
▤ Send a fax to 44 (0) 1865 314091
▢ Visit the Heinemann Bookshop at www.heinemann.co.uk/library to browse our catalogue and order online.

First published in Great Britain by Heinemann Library,
Halley Court, Jordan Hill, Oxford OX2 8EJ,
a division of Reed Educational and Professional Publishing Ltd.
Heinemann is a registered trademark of Reed Educational and Professional Publishing Ltd.

OXFORD MELBOURNE AUCKLAND
JOHANNESBURG BLANTYRE GABORONE
IBADAN PORTSMOUTH (NH) USA CHICAGO

Designed by AMR
Illustrated by Art Construction
Originated by Ambassador Litho Ltd
Printed by Wing King Tong

ISBN 0 431 10490 5 (hardback)   ISBN 0 431 10495 6 (paperback)
06 05 04 03 02   07 06 05 04 03
10 9 8 7 6 5 4 3 2 1   10 9 8 7 6 5 4 3 2 1

British Library Cataloguing in Publication Data
Reid, Struan
  Christopher Columbus. – (Groundbreakers)
  1.Colon, Cristobal, 1451–1506 2.Explorers – Spain
  Biography – Juvenile literature
  I.Title
  970'.015'092

Acknowledgements
The publishers would like to thank the following for permission to reproduce photographs:
Bridgeman: p. 27; Bridgeman/British Museum: p. 33; Bridgeman/Koninklijk Museum, Belgium: p. 25; Bridgeman/Metropolitan Museum of Art, New York: p. 4; Bridgeman/Musee des Beaux-arts Andre Malraux: p. 38; Bridgeman/Museu de Marinha, Lisbon: p. 9; Bridgeman/Prado, Madrid: p. 10; Bridgeman/Royal Geographical Society: p. 41; British Museum: p. 13; Colin Dixon: pp. 11, 30; Corbis: pp. 15, 34, 39; Dave Saunders: p. 40; Hereford Cathedral: p. 5; Mansell/Timepix: pp. 6, 37; Hulton: p. 18; Mary Evans: pp. 7, 12, 14, 17, 19, 20, 32; Michael Holford: p. 23; National Maritime Museum: p. 29; Robert Harding: p. 21; Travel Ink: p. 36; Travel Ink/David Toase: p. 26; Travel Ink/Simon Reddy: pp. 22, 24; Woodfall Wild Images: pp. 8, 16.

Cover photograph reproduced with permission of Bridgeman.

Every effort has been made to contact copyright holders of any material reproduced in this book. Any omissions will be rectified in subsequent printings if notice is given to the publishers.

Our thanks to Christopher Gibb for his comments in the preparation of this book.

Disclaimer
All the Internet addresses (URLs) given in this book were valid at the time of going to press. However, due to the dynamic nature of the Internet, some addresses may have changed, or sites may have ceased to exist since publication. While the author and publishers regret any inconvenience this may cause readers, no responsibility for any such changes can be accepted by either the author or the publishers.

Any words appearing in the text in bold, **like this**, are explained in the glossary.

Contents

The shock of the new

People today can travel in aeroplanes from one side of the world to the other in less than a day. Our messages travel thousands of miles in seconds, bounced off satellites in the sky. We are surrounded with information about the countries of the world and their inhabitants.

Five hundred years ago, when Christopher Columbus lived, people had a completely different idea of the world. Most people travelled only very short distances to their nearest town, usually only on market days. Merchants and traders who travelled further afield told stories of mysterious foreign lands, but nobody knew much about them.

During the 15th century this limited picture of the world began to change. European explorers were beginning to travel further and further away from their homelands. They were searching for a sea route to the East, where they hoped to find great riches – gold, silver, precious stones and spices. Explorers returned with accounts of the lands they found, and mapmakers could then draw more accurate maps of the world, with fewer blank spaces.

Map of the known world in the 15th century.

Inspiration

One of the greatest of these early explorers was Christopher Columbus. As a boy he had been inspired to sail to **Cathay** (China) after reading the account of the travels in the 13th century of Marco Polo, a Venetian merchant. In 1492, Columbus and his small crew set sail from Spain in three tiny ships, with no clear idea of where they were going or what they would find. What they did find at the end of their journey was an entire continent now called America. Although Vikings from Scandinavia had sailed there 500 years earlier (see box, page 40), it had been long forgotten by Europeans. The lands Columbus 'discovered' were rich, fertile and ruled by astonishing civilizations.

True impact

Columbus never really understood the importance of his discovery: the 'New World' eventually brought fabulous riches into Europe, but at a price. Europeans regarded these lands as theirs to **conquer** and plunder, and in so doing they destroyed ancient civilizations that had existed there for millennia.

In Columbus's words:

'Seven years passed in discussions [planning his expedition] and nine in the enterprise itself. Remarkable and memorable events took place in those years, which no one could have conceived beforehand.'

(Taken from a letter written in 1500 by Columbus to the king and queen of Spain)

A portrait of Christopher Columbus by an Italian artist called Sebastiano del Piombo. It shows Columbus at the height of his fame, but was painted in 1519, 13 years after his death.

Columbus's early life

Cristoforo (Christopher) Colombo was born in 1451 in the north Italian port of Genoa, first child of Domenico, a wool weaver, and Susanna. Christopher was followed by two brothers – Bartolomeo and Diego (also known as Giacomo) – and a sister, Bianchinetta; a further brother, Giovanni, died very young.

The family was poor and Domenico could afford to give his children only a basic education. While they were still young, the children started working in their father's weaving business. The boys cleaned the wool and their mother and sister spun the wool into yarn. Their father would then weave the wool into lengths of cloth.

Genova la Superba

When Christopher and his brothers and sister were growing up, Genoa was an independent **city-state** ruled by a handful of powerful families. Italy at that time was not a united country and was made up of a number of city-states. Genoa was one of the most important and richest centres of trade in Europe, known as *Genova la Superba* (Genoa the Superb).

A view of the Italian port of Genoa. This engraving, from a 15th-century book called The Nuremberg Chronicles, *shows the city as it would have looked when Columbus was young.*

The city's streets were lined with the marble palaces of noble families and rich merchants. The port was crowded with ships bringing silks and spices from the Far East, which were then sold to merchants from across Europe. The city was famous for its mapmakers, **navigators** and shipbuilders. It was also famous for its bankers, who opened branches of their banks in all the main cities of Europe.

At the end of a tiring day in his father's workshop, Christopher would go down to the docks to watch the ships unloading their valuable **cargoes**. He heard stories from the sailors about far-away lands and must have longed to join them on journeys across the sea.

This 16th-century painting shows harvesters gathering peppercorns in the **Spice Islands**, major destinations for expeditions from Europe.

TRADE BARRIERS

In 1453, the Turks captured the ancient Greek city of Constantinople (present-day Istanbul), gaining control of all the overland trade routes between Europe and the Far East. As a result, the silks and spices from the East that the Europeans loved so much became extremely expensive. The Italian ports of Genoa and Venice then became the two main entry points for these goods into Europe and grew very rich from the trade.

In a poet's words:

'So many are the Genoese
And so extended everywhere,
They go to any place they please
And recreate their city there.'

(Taken from a poem written by a 15th-century poet known as the Anonymous of Genoa)

A new life

Little is known about Columbus's youth, although he probably worked as a sailor from the age of about fourteen. In 1476, aged 25, Columbus joined the crew of a merchant ship bound for northern Europe. However, they were attacked by another ship and sank 9.5 kilometres (6 miles) off Portugal. Columbus managed to swim ashore and travelled north to the capital city Lisbon, where his brother Bartolomeo had already settled.

New skills and ideas

Lisbon was then the most important centre of exploration in the whole of Europe. Bartolomeo was a successful mapmaker in the city and Christopher probably joined him in his work. Determined to be an explorer, he taught himself mathematics, geography and **astronomy** and quickly earned a reputation as a skilled seaman and mapmaker.

In Columbus's words:

'During this time I have made it my business to read all that has been written on geography, history, philosophy and other sciences.'

(Taken from a letter written by Columbus in 1501 to the king and queen of Spain)

The city of Lisbon today. It was built on a number of hills overlooking the River Tagus, which leads directly to the Atlantic Ocean. Columbus developed his mapmaking skills while living in Lisbon.

Dona Felipa

In about 1480, aged 29, Columbus married Felipa Perestrello e Moniz, the daughter of a Portuguese nobleman and governor of the island of Porto Santo near Madeira. The young couple went to live on Porto Santo and in 1481, Felipa gave birth to a son, Diego. Their marriage lasted only a short time as Felipa died, probably in 1483.

Columbus never married again, but he did have another son, Ferdinand (or Fernando), with the woman he lived with for the rest of his life – Beatriz de Arana.

A new direction

While living on Porto Santo, Columbus worked out a plan to sail to Japan by travelling westward across the **Ocean Sea** (Atlantic Ocean). He thought he would be able to sail uninterrupted to the Far East, where he would find the silks, spices and other luxuries so popular in Europe. Columbus's maps suggested that the journey would cover only 4800 kilometres (3000 miles), but the actual distance is more than 16,000 kilometres (10,000 miles)!

To organize the expedition, Columbus needed the **backing** (sponsorship) of King John II of Portugal. At the time, overland routes were closed to Europeans and in their quest for a sea route to the Far East, all Portuguese expeditions followed the west coast of Africa in search of a way east. Columbus believed his westward route would be quicker, but royal advisers thought this idea was eccentric and in 1485 refused backing. Columbus decided to try his luck in Spain.

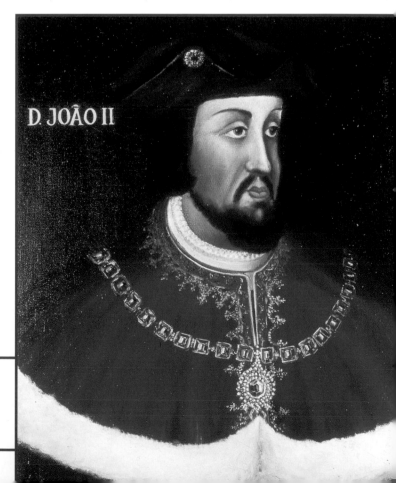

D. JOÃO II

King John II of Portugal (who reigned 1481–95) sponsored many expeditions from Lisbon to the East.

Royal support

In 1485, Columbus left Portugal with his five-year-old son Diego and crossed into southern Spain. Their first stop was the **monastery** of La Rábida near the small port of Palos de la Frontera. They were tired and hot, so Columbus asked the monks for food and water for his young son. Incredibly, stopping at the monastery started a chain of events that would change his life.

Influential contacts

While Columbus rested at La Rábida he spoke to the **Prior**, Juan Perez, who listened carefully to his plans and ideas for exploration. Perez introduced Columbus to another monk, Antonio de Marchena, who was not only a well-known **astronomer**, but had also been confessor to Queen Isabella of Spain.

Leaving Diego behind at La Rábida to be educated by the monks, Columbus moved to the city of Seville. Using the monks' contacts, he was soon introduced to the Duke of Medina Celi, a rich Spanish nobleman and shipowner. The Duke knew the King and Queen and was sure they would be interested in Columbus's expedition plans.

This 19th-century painting shows Christopher Columbus and his son Diego arriving exhausted at the monastery of La Rábida. Their arrival there would eventually change the course of world history.

In 1486, Queen Isabella ordered Columbus to present his plans at the **royal court** in Cordoba. However, her preoccupation at this time was not exploration, but the **conquest** of the southern Spanish kingdom of Granada from its **Muslim** rulers. Although Columbus argued his case repeatedly, eventually, in 1490, the royal commissioners refused **backing**.

Getting ahead

In 1492, Granada fell to the Christian armies of Ferdinand and Isabella and the Queen was now able to turn her attention to Columbus's plans. She knew that the expeditions of Spain's great rival Portugal were getting closer and closer to the riches of India and it was vital that Spain should find her own sea route to the East. Isabella gave Columbus her backing and at long last the expedition that he had hoped for could begin.

ISABELLA AND FERDINAND

The two largest kingdoms in Spain, Castile and Aragon, were joined in 1469 when Queen Isabella of Castile (1451–1504) married King Ferdinand of Aragon (1452–1516). Spain became a united kingdom when Granada was finally captured in 1492. Under the rule of the two monarchs, Spain became the most powerful nation in Europe.

In Columbus's words:

'Your Highnesses commanded me that, with a sufficient fleet, I should go to the said parts of India.'

(Taken from *The Journal of Christopher Columbus*, written by his son Ferdinand)

The Court of the Lions in the Alhambra palace. King Ferdinand and Queen Isabella took over this palace in Granada when they defeated the Muslim kingdom there in 1492.

Columbus, now 41 years old, felt he would have been too old to embark upon such an ambitious expedition in a few more years. Letters were sent from the king and queen of Spain granting him all the ships and equipment he would need. They also promised to give him a tenth of all the 'gold, silver, pearls, gems, spices and other **merchandise**' he was expected to find. They would keep the rest.

Ships and crew

Columbus returned to the port of Palos as soon as he could, to begin preparations for the expedition. But royal advisers ordered the authorities in Palos to organize everything – three ships, crews, **ammunition** and supplies – in just ten days, and to pay for two of the ships themselves. Such demands built up great resentment in Palos against Columbus and his expedition. Many people also thought he was mad to attempt to cross the **Ocean Sea** to reach the East.

> ### In Columbus's words:
>
> *'And I departed from the city of Granada on the twelfth day of the month of May in … 1492 … and came to the town of Palos, which is a port of the sea, where I made ready three ships ….'*
>
> (Taken from *The Journal of Christopher Columbus*)

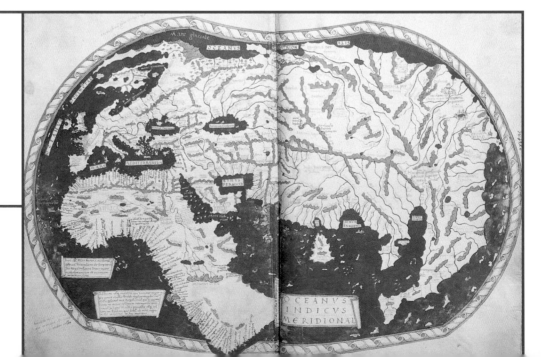

A map drawn in about 1490, showing the world as Columbus would have known it.

Helping hand

Some people, however, were prepared to support Columbus, including a number of bankers and merchants who were tempted by the promised riches. Another was a local shipowner, Martín Alonso Pinzón, who supplied two of the ships and recruited many sailors for the expedition. Some were criminals, specially released from prison, given a last chance to win fame and fortune.

The ships were loaded with supplies for the journey – barrels of water and beer, flour, rice, dried biscuits and beans, and even live chickens and pigs. Ropes and canvas were needed for repairs and guns to protect them from attack. After ten weeks of preparations, the ships were ready to sail.

*A statue at Palos de la Frontera of the Spanish **navigator** Martín Pinzón (c.1441–93), regarded by many as the real hero of Columbus's expedition.*

PORTUGUESE RIVALS

In August 1487, King John II of Portugal sent out an expedition of three ships from Lisbon. It was led by Bartolomeu Dias (c.1450–1500), who had been instructed to open the sea route round Africa. Towards the end of 1487 the expedition sailed round the southern tip of Africa. This was named the Cape of Good Hope, for a sea route to the riches of India and the East had been found.

13

Life on board

YOU CAN
FOLLOW
COLUMBUS'S
FIRST
EXPEDITION
ON THE MAP
ON PAGES
42–3.

At dawn on the morning of 3 August 1492, the three ships sailed quietly out of Palos to a sandbank called Saltes where they waited for a wind to carry them westward. At 8 a.m. a gentle breeze blew up and filled the ships' sails and, like great white birds, they were soon on their way, heading south-west for the Canary Islands.

An engraving showing Columbus officially taking his leave from King Ferdinand and Queen Isabella. Isabella was the main driving force behind the Spanish expeditions.

Three small ships

Columbus's expedition consisted of three small ships, all weighing less than 100 tonnes and none longer than 24 metres. Their names are now among the most famous in the history of exploration: the *Santa Maria*, the *Niña* and the *Pinta*.

The *Santa Maria* was classed as a *nao*, a heavy **cargo** ship. She was the **flagship** of the expedition and Columbus sailed on her as captain-general of the fleet. Also sailing in her were a number of royal officials, whose job was to take charge of the cargoes of exotic **merchandise** they hoped to bring back.

The *Niña* was really called the *Santa Clara*, but as she had once been owned by the Niño family of Palos, crew members called her *Niña*. The captain of the ship was Vincente, brother of Martín Pinzón. The *Niña* was a type of ship called a caravel, popular with Portuguese explorers. Its long, low and narrow **hull** made it strong, but nimble.

The *Pinta* was another caravel. She had three square sails, unlike the *Niña* which had triangular-shaped 'lateen' sails. Pinzón sailed in her as captain while his other brother, Francisco, was master.

A mid-17th century engraving depicting Columbus using navigational instruments.

Daily routine

Some of the officers, including Columbus, would have had their own cabins on board the ships, but everyone else slept on the lower decks on straw-filled sacks. Food was probably cooked on a **brazier** on the upper deck. There was little fresh food and meals were usually gruel or soup made from grain, salted meat and dry biscuits. Each day was divided into six 'watches' of four hours each. A **lookout** always kept watch high up in the **crow's-nest** on the ship's main mast.

Sailing westward

YOU CAN FOLLOW COLUMBUS'S FIRST EXPEDITION ON THE MAP ON PAGES 42–3.

After years of planning and weeks of preparations the expedition was finally on its way. Almost immediately after their departure from Spain, problems broke out. While many believed in Columbus's abilities, others did not and still doubted the wisdom of the expedition.

Delayed in the Canaries

On the fourth day from Spain, the **rudder** on the *Pinta* broke. The fleet managed to limp into harbour in the Canary Islands, but it took a month before the damage was repaired. Columbus was certain that the owner of the *Pinta*, Cristobal Quintero, was plotting against him and had sabotaged the ship. Valuable time had been wasted and the crews were growing impatient.

At last, at midday on 6 September, the ships set sail again. Three days later they had completely lost sight of all land and were entering unknown waters. The further they travelled out to sea, the more nervous the men became – many feared they would never see their families again.

A view of the Canary Islands today. Lying off the west coast of Africa, the group of islands was a vital stopping point for ships sailing from Europe on their way south and west.

The Santa Maria, *the* Niña *and the* Pinta *on the high seas, sailing across unknown waters. Battered by winds and towering waves, they finally reached land more than two months later.*

First sighting

At about 10 p.m. on 11 October, Columbus thought he could see a light flickering ahead of them 'like a little wax candle rising and falling'. He called out to two of his officers on the *Santa Maria*, but they could see nothing. At 2 a.m. the following morning, though, the **lookout** on the *Pinta* sighted land and a cannon was fired to announce the news.

At dawn the ships sailed into a bay and dropped anchor, 70 days after leaving Spain. On the beach, local people watched with amazement as Columbus and several officers rowed towards them. Columbus leapt out and dropped to his knees, giving thanks to God and claiming the land for the king and queen of Spain. The land they had reached was one of the islands now known as the Bahamas. The local people called it Guanahani, but Columbus renamed it San Salvador.

TWO DISTANCES

Columbus decided that two counts should be kept of the distance covered each day. One would be an accurate one for himself while the other would give a reduced distance for the crew. He did this 'in order that the men should not be discouraged or frightened by the excessive length of the journey'. He also nailed a gold coin to the mast of the *Santa Maria*, to be given to the first man who sighted land.

Exploration of the Indies

The people who lived on the island were the Tainos. Columbus, however, was so convinced he had reached the Indies near India, and that beyond them must lie Japan and **Cathay**, that he called the local people 'Indians'.

A tour of the islands

Columbus and his men were given a warm, but guarded, welcome by the Tainos, who exchanged food for some of the gifts that the Spaniards had brought from Spain, such as small bells, knives and glass beads. Potatoes and **cassava** plants were grown as food on the islands and the people smoked the dry leaves of tobacco plants. All these were unknown to the Europeans.

> ### In Columbus's words:
>
> *'As soon as day broke, there came to the shore many of these men, all youths ... all of good height, very handsome people.'*
>
> (From the log book of the *Santa Maria*, dated 13 October 1492)

After two days on San Salvador, Columbus sailed round the island to some of the neighbouring islands, later reporting: 'I saw so many islands that I could not decide to which I would go first.' He gave each a new name and everywhere he landed he set up a Christian cross. On 28 October, he reached Cuba, which he was certain must be Japan.

The lack of gold on San Salvador was a great disappointment to the Spaniards, but having learnt a few words of Tainos language, they heard of an island 'where ... the people gather gold on the beach by candles at night'. This rumour was enough to make Pinzón desert the expedition and take the *Pinta* in search of gold.

A woodcut illustration of 1493 showing Columbus touring the islands. The European artist has shown, on the left, a local ruler dressed as a European king.

An engraving showing Christopher Columbus on the island of Hispaniola (Haiti), where he founded the first Spanish settlement in the Americas.

Home from home

On 6 December 1492, Columbus reached the island now known as Haiti. It reminded him so much of Spain he named it Hispaniola. On Christmas Eve, as Columbus lay sleeping in his cabin, the *Santa Maria* ran aground on Hispaniola. The ship had to be abandoned, but Columbus saw in this disaster a sign from God. He named the site Puerto de la Navidad (Christmas Port) and left a group of 39 men there to build a fort from the boat **timbers**. The rest of the men transferred to the *Niña*.

YOU CAN FOLLOW COLUMBUS'S FIRST EXPEDITION ON THE MAP ON PAGES 42–3.

THE MEETING OF CULTURES

When Columbus first left Spain, Ferdinand and Isabella gave him strict instructions to treat any local people he might meet with respect. These good intentions did not last long. Within 50 years of Columbus's arrival, most of the local people on the islands had been exterminated through warfare, disease and **persecution**, while others were sold into slavery.

The return journey

YOU CAN FOLLOW COLUMBUS'S FIRST EXPEDITION ON THE MAP ON PAGES 42–3.

On 4 January 1493, Columbus set sail on the *Niña* bound for Spain. On board were six Tainos men and a collection of birds, fruits and plants, which were to be presented to King Ferdinand and Queen Isabella.

Across the Ocean Sea

As the *Niña* sailed away from Navidad, her crew spotted the *Pinta*. The two ships met and Pinzón came aboard the *Niña*. According to Columbus, Pinzón gave him 'invented excuses and false arguments' to explain his desertion. Although still very angry with Pinzón, Columbus preserved the peace.

The two ships sailed towards Spain together and were halfway back by 9 February. However, a great storm blew up which lasted for three whole days and nights. The two ships were tossed from side to side and eventually were separated from each other. When the storm died down the crews of both ships assumed the other had been lost and so they continued their journeys back to Spain separately.

A late 15th-century illustration of a sea creature off the coast of Hispaniola. Many sailors at this time believed that terrifying monsters lurked beneath the waves, waiting to devour them.

In Columbus's words:

'Here he began to experience heavy seas and stormy weather, and he says if the caravel had not been very good and well equipped he would have feared to be lost.'

(From *The Journal of Christopher Columbus* describing the return journey)

During the course of the expedition, Columbus and Pinzón grew very suspicious of each other. It was the **lookout** on Pinzón's ship, the *Pinta*, who had first spotted land and Pinzón had deserted the expedition to look for gold. For years after Pinzón's death, his family and friends suggested that it was he, and not Columbus, who was really the hero of the expedition.

Quiet return

On 4 March 1493, the *Niña* sailed into the harbour at Lisbon. Columbus reported his findings to King John II of Portugal. Portugal and Spain were bitter rivals in trade and exploration. The Portuguese, particularly jealous of Columbus's success despite their having refused him **backing** in 1485, nearly had him murdered.

On 15 March, Columbus and the *Niña* sailed back into the Spanish port of Palos. Pinzón, on the *Pinta*, had already reached northern Spain in February and broken the news of the expedition's success. He arrived in Palos shortly after Columbus, but fell gravely ill and died a few days later. With Pinzón dead, Columbus then became the hero of the moment.

A view of Lisbon today, looking towards the harbour. It has been an important port for centuries.

A hero's welcome

Columbus had been away seven months and although very excited about his discoveries, he was also exhausted. So he rested for two weeks at the **monastery** of La Rábida and talked with **Prior** Perez, who had encouraged his exploration. He was also reunited with his sons Diego and Ferdinand, who had been cared for in nearby Seville.

Royal reception

Ferdinand and Isabella summoned Columbus to their **royal court** in Barcelona in north-eastern Spain to speak of his journey. He had to travel from the south to the north of Spain, so he organized a spectacular procession to publicize his great achievement.

At the front of the procession came the six Tainos dressed in their gold ornaments, followed by souvenirs such as colourful parrots in gilded cages, and exotic plants. Columbus rode on horseback at the end, waving to the hundreds of cheering people along the route.

Barcelona Cathedral, where a celebration mass would have been held to mark Columbus's return.

When they finally reached Barcelona, 'all the court and city came out'. Columbus was ushered into the audience chamber where he knelt before the King and Queen. They ordered him to rise and sit in a place of honour beside the Queen. He told them all about the expedition and the adventures along the way while the Tainos and souvenirs were shown off.

Following Columbus's triumphant presentation at the royal court at Barcelona, the six Tainos stayed with him throughout the time he was in Spain. Five of them returned to their island on Columbus's second expedition, while one remained behind at the Spanish royal court where he died two years later.

Golden promises

Everyone in Barcelona was sure Columbus had found a new route to the **Indies**. Columbus pointed to the gold ornaments worn by the Tainos and said that much more would be found. Impressed by these promises of great future riches, royal **backing** was given to a second expedition and Columbus was appointed 'Governor of the islands that he has discovered in the Indies'.

This gold Spanish coin shows the heads of Ferdinand and Isabella. Columbus would have taken coins like this on his voyages.

In Columbus's words:

'In conclusion, … their Highnesses can see that I will give them as much gold as they may need, if their Highnesses will render me very slight assistance; presently, I will give them spices and cotton, as much as their Highnesses shall command ….'

(Written 15 February 1493 by Columbus in a letter describing the results of his first voyage)

A second expedition

Although he had no real proof of it, Columbus's tales of abundant gold on the islands bewitched many of his listeners. Young men in their hundreds begged him to take them on his next voyage. Unlike his first expedition, this journey gave him no difficulty in recruiting volunteers.

Preparations for settlement

The King and Queen appointed Don Juan de Fonseca, Archdeacon of Seville, to the new position of Superintendant of the Affairs of the **Indies**. It was his job to organize all the preparations for the second expedition. In a few months, he managed to equip 17 ships with enough supplies to last 6 months and recruited 1200 seamen. Among them was Columbus's younger brother Diego.

Guadaloupe monastery, where Columbus stayed after the celebrations for his return to Spain.

Pope Alexander VI, painted in about 1506 by the famous Italian artist Titian. At the Treaty of Tordesillas in 1494, the Pope divided the known world between Spain and Portugal.

The official instructions for the second expedition were dated 29 May 1493. They stated that the main purpose of the expedition was to be to **convert** the local people to Christianity. Columbus had described them as '**idolators**' (people who worship idols). Ferdinand and Isabella strongly believed it was their royal duty to convert all the people who lived in the lands ruled by them to the **Catholic** religion. Among the travellers were Father Bernado Buil, chaplain to the fleet, and four other priests.

The second important objective was to establish a trading colony. Columbus was also instructed to make detailed maps of all the islands. A third, and perhaps most important, objective was to find gold.

Builders and farmers were also recruited, and brought with them seeds, plants and farm animals. This was to be a full-scale expedition of **colonization**. Most of the men came from the southern Spanish region of Andalucia and some had been on Columbus's first voyage. Soldiers, cavalrymen and their horses were also on board, for this was to be an expedition of **conquest** as well as of trade.

WORDS OF DOUBT

While most people were willing to believe Columbus really had found a sea route to the riches of the East, some were not so sure. One of them, an Italian living in Spain called Pietro Martire d'Anghiera, studied Columbus's accounts of his first journey. From these he concluded that it was highly unlikely that Columbus had gone as far as Asia. D'Anghiera believed Columbus had found a 'New World' unknown to Europeans, but did not realize the islands fringed an entirely new continent.

A gloomy return

On 25 September 1493, the fleet of ships set sail from the southern Spanish port of Cadiz. Their first stop was the Canary Islands where they took on board more food and other supplies.

The docks at the port of Cadiz in southern Spain. Cadiz is one of the oldest cities in Spain and its port has been one of the busiest and most important for thousands of years.

A quick crossing

On this second expedition Columbus chose a more southerly route. The ships had to battle through one storm along the way, but for most of the journey the crossing was smooth and quick. On Sunday 3 November, just 22 days after leaving the Canaries, the **lookouts** sighted an island to the south of Hispaniola. Columbus named it Dominica, which is the Spanish for 'Sunday'.

Columbus explored further islands around Dominica. He named one of these Guadeloupe after the famous **monastery** in Spain. As the ships lay offshore, one of his captains, Diego Marquez, disobeyed orders and went ashore. He quickly got lost in the thick forests covering the island and search parties had to be sent out to find him.

YOU CAN FOLLOW COLUMBUS'S SECOND EXPEDITION ON THE MAP ON PAGES 42–3.

Telling tales

As the men hacked their way through the **vegetation**, they saw many beautiful trees and sweet-smelling plants that were unknown in Europe. On their return to the ships, they also claimed to have seen some terrifying sights on the island. Guadeloupe was populated by the fierce Carib people, who were greatly feared by the more peaceful Tainos and Arawaks of the other islands. The Spanish sailors returned to their ships with stories of human limbs hanging from trees and captured young Tainos children being fattened up for cooking.

Marquez was eventually found and the ships sailed on. The expedition reached the eastern coast of Hispaniola on 22 November and five days later landed at Navidad. Far from being greeted by the settlers, they were met by an eerie silence and the sight of the blackened ruins of the wooden fort. They learned from local Tainos that the settlers had all been **massacred** by a raiding party of Arawaks from the centre of the island.

Many of the plants, fruits and vegetables, such as tobacco, pineapples and potatoes, that Columbus and his men found on the islands, were exported back to Spain. They eventually had a great effect on European society. The pineapple was highly prized by kings while the potato changed the farming economies of Europe for ever.

A late 16th-century illustration of a pineapple. Following the European discovery of the Americas, many new fruits, vegetables and other plants were taken back to Europe.

Success turns to disaster

A woodcut illustration showing the destruction of the Spanish settlement of Navidad. Columbus was told that the Chief Caonabo of the Arawaks attacked and burned the settlement.

Columbus was horrified to see the ruins of Navidad, but refused to be discouraged. He ordered the fleet to sail on around Hispaniola in search of a new site for a settlement, near to where Columbus believed they would find gold.

A new settlement

The journey round Hispaniola was extremely difficult. They were sailing against screaming winds and strong currents and after 25 days they had only managed to cover 48 kilometres (30 miles). Eventually, on 2 January 1494, they found a bay where they could shelter. Columbus sent men ashore to start building a new settlement. He named it Isabella in honour of the queen who had given him so much support in 'the enterprise of the **Indies**'.

Columbus and a small force of armed men explored the interior of Hispaniola. They crossed a range of mountains and saw a vast, beautiful plain stretching out before them, which Columbus named Vega Real, or Royal Plain. When he returned to Isabella, the settlement was in chaos. The men complained the site was unhealthy, as many had fallen ill. They also complained they had been tricked into joining the expedition – where was the gold Columbus had promised?

YOU CAN FOLLOW COLUMBUS'S SECOND EXPEDITION ON THE MAP ON PAGES 42–3.

Fighting to survive

To prevent a **mutiny**, Columbus had the main troublemakers arrested. Leaving his brother Diego in charge of the settlement, he left to explore Cuba, which he still believed was Japan. On his return to Isabella, Columbus found that his brother Bartolomeo had arrived from Spain with fresh supplies. His joy at the reunion was short-lived – a large group of Arawaks had gathered on the Vega Real to attack the settlement. Columbus led a small army out from the settlement and destroyed the invaders.

This victory could not hide the fact that the expedition was in disarray. News of the problems had reached the ears of Ferdinand and Isabella in Spain, who were becoming very concerned. Columbus decided he must return to Spain himself in order to clear his name.

The Battle of Vega Real in 1494 was the first real confrontation between the Spanish **colonists** and the local people. Columbus led a small force of 200 foot soldiers, 20 cavalrymen and 20 hunting dogs against several thousand Arawak warriors. This was the first time the local people had seen horses and guns.

In Columbus's words:

'Evil words arose in Spain and belittlement of the enterprise which had been begun there, because I had not at once dispatched ships laden with gold ....'

(From a letter written by Columbus in his own defence to the king and queen of Spain)

Engraving of 1594 by Theodore de Bry showing a rebellion of Native Americans against Spanish settlers. At the Battle of Vega Real, local people tried to drive the Spaniards off their land.

The third expedition

YOU CAN FOLLOW COLUMBUS'S THIRD EXPEDITION ON THE MAP ON PAGES 42–3.

Columbus left Hispaniola for Spain with two ships on 10 March 1496. For more than two years he had struggled with all sorts of problems on the island. One of his main failures, in the eyes of his Spanish backers, was that he had so far found very little gold or **merchandise** to take back to Spain.

In defence

Columbus arrived in Cadiz on 11 June 1496 to a quiet reception. He hurried north to meet the King and Queen in the city of Burgos. A royal enquiry had already cleared Columbus of any wrongdoing on the expedition. Ferdinand and Isabella also chose not to believe the stories that were being told against him. They had enough confidence in Columbus to give **backing** to a third expedition. However, others plotted against him and it took two years before his new expedition was ready to sail.

Eight ships sailed in the third expedition. Two ships left in January 1498 and sailed directly to Hispaniola. The other six left four months later from the Canaries. Three of these sailed to the Cape Verde Islands off the west coast of Africa. Travelling south towards the Equator, the ships entered the **doldrums**. With no winds or currents to carry them along, they lay stranded for eight days under the blazing sun.

Burgos Cathedral in northern Spain. The King and Queen would spend the hot summer months in the cooler cities to the north of the country.

At last a small breeze carried them further westward. On 31 July, three mountain peaks were spotted in the distance that Columbus named Trinidad, in honour of the **Holy Trinity**. The ships sailed on to the Gulf of Paria and along a shoreline, which Columbus thought must be that of another island. In fact, they were sailing along the coast of South America near present-day Venezuela.

Clapped in irons

While Columbus had been in Spain, his brothers Diego and Bartolomeo had abandoned the unhealthy site at Isabella and founded a new settlement they named Santo Domingo. When Columbus arrived at Santo Domingo, he found the settlers fighting among themselves. He again tried to impose law and order and several settlers were **executed**.

Alarmed at this latest twist of events, Ferdinand and Isabella sent a royal official called Francisco de Bobadilla to investigate. Upon reaching Santo Domingo in August 1500, he found the settlers still fighting and had Columbus and his brothers arrested and shipped back to Spain in chains.

In Columbus's words:

'Here by God's will I have brought under the dominion of our Sovereigns a new world ... I should be judged as a captain ... No pirate treated a merchant like this!'

(From a letter written by Columbus while under arrest)

Illustration of Columbus and his ships arriving at Trinidad, with an inset portrait of Columbus on the left.

In disgrace

'There go the sons of the Admiral of Mosquitos, of the man who discovered the lands of vanity and fraud, the cemetery of Castilian noblemen.' People of Seville shouted out insults like this to Columbus's two sons, Diego and Ferdinand. They were being brought up at the Spanish **royal court** in Seville, as their father was being returned to Spain a prisoner.

Christopher Columbus refused to have his chains removed until he was brought before King Ferdinand and Queen Isabella of Spain. He always kept his chains and even wanted to be buried in them when he died.

Fallen angels

The ship reached Cadiz in November 1500 but six weeks passed before Columbus received a royal summons to meet the king and queen. When he entered their **audience chamber** in Granada, Columbus bowed low before Ferdinand and Isabella. They responded with the same kindness and respect as before and his chains were removed.

Ferdinand and Isabella reassured him he would be restored as **governor** of the **Indies**. But after many months, he heard that he was to be replaced by Nicolás de Ovando, who set sail from Spain in February 1502 with a fleet of 30 ships and 2500 men.

One last chance

However, the King and Queen gave Columbus permission to lead a fourth expedition to find a westward passage to India, **Cathay** and the **Spice Islands**. He set sail from Cadiz in four old ships on 9 May 1502, this time accompanied by his second son Ferdinand, who was twelve years old.

VASCO DA GAMA (C.1460–1524)

In July 1497, as Columbus was still trying to find a westward route to India, a fleet of 4 ships and 170 men set sail south from Lisbon in Portugal. It was led by a Portuguese nobleman called Vasco da Gama. After ten months at sea, the fleet finally reached Calicut on the west coast of India. The Portuguese had won the race to the Indies.

*A portrait of the Portuguese explorer Vasco da Gama, the first European to sail round the coast of Africa to India. The discovery of this route started **colonization** of the Far East by Europeans.*

JOHN CABOT (C.1450–C.1498)

After Columbus's supposed achievement in reaching the 'Indies', King Henry VII of England gave **backing** to another Italian, Giovanni Caboto (John Cabot), to sail across the Atlantic. In 1497, he reached the coast of Canada, which he believed to be Asia. He embarked on another expedition in 1498 but never returned.

Endless wanderings

YOU CAN FOLLOW COLUMBUS'S FOURTH EXPEDITION ON THE MAP ON PAGES 42–3.

Columbus was 51 years old when he set out on his fourth expedition. He was in a great deal of pain, suffering from **arthritis** and poor eyesight. Although he had been treated kindly by Ferdinand and Isabella, he still felt humiliated and angry that he had been replaced as **governor**.

An unwelcome visitor

On 29 June 1502, Columbus and his small fleet reached the new settlement of Santo Domingo. He had been refused permission by Ferdinand and Isabella to disembark there, as they were afraid he would pick a fight with the new governor, Nicolás de Ovando. He continued westward to find a passage to India. By the end of July he had reached the coast of Central America where he exchanged goods with the local people.

THE DEATH OF BOBADILLA

At Santo Domingo, Columbus sent a message warning that a violent storm was heading for Hispaniola. However, ignoring this warning, about 26 ships still left for Spain. All but one were destroyed in the storm and their crews drowned. Among these lost men was Juan de Bobadilla, Columbus's former jailor and sworn enemy. The single ship to survive was one carrying Columbus's possessions.

Between mid-August and mid-September, as they were sailing along the coast of the country now known as Honduras, Columbus's fleet ran into violent storms. Columbus recorded in his log book that 'the ships lay exposed to the weather, with sails torn, and anchors, rigging, cables, boats and many of the stores lost' for 28 days.

Aerial photograph of the coast of Honduras, taken in 1998 soon after Hurricane Mitch had blown across the land. Columbus had to battle against terrible storms off the coast of Honduras.

Veragua

They spent months sailing back and forth along the coastline of Central America, trying in vain to reach the **Indies**. On around 6 January 1503, unable to go any further, the ships dropped anchor at the mouth of a river and the men rowed ashore. The local people called this land Veragua and today it is known as Panama.

With few supplies and fearing attack by local warriors, the fleet headed south to Santo Domingo. Two ships were leaking so badly they had to be abandoned. The men crowded onto the remaining two ships. As they sank lower and lower into the water, it became clear these ships were not going to last the journey. Finally, on 25 June, the ships ran aground on Jamaica.

Illustration of Columbus landing at Veragua (Panama), with a portrait of his brother Bartolomeo on the right.

Mutiny and rescue

Columbus and his men were stranded on Jamaica. The two ships were unfit to sail again but the crew built straw-roofed huts on the decks for shelter.

A photograph of the coast of Jamaica today. Columbus and his crew were shipwrecked in similar surroundings for a whole year.

A long wait

Columbus hoped it would not be too long before they were rescued. However, no gold had been found on Jamaica, and very few ships passed in their direction. In the end, they were stranded a whole year on Jamaica.

When the last of the food had been eaten, a young officer called Diego Mendez took three sailors and journeyed inland. Some local Tainos people they met exchanged fresh food for Spanish goods, but others grew restless at the Spaniards' presence.

A TERRIBLE WARNING

When the Tainos refused to supply them with any more food, Columbus devised a trick. Knowing that an **eclipse** of the Moon would take place on the next night, he warned the Tainos that this would be a sign of God's anger. When the Moon disappeared from sight as predicted, the terrified Tainos begged Columbus to restore it to the skies and agreed to renew their supplies of food!

YOU CAN FOLLOW COLUMBUS'S FOURTH EXPEDITION ON THE MAP ON PAGES 42–3.

Great gamble

Realizing the expedition was in great danger, Columbus persuaded Mendez and another officer to paddle a Tainos canoe across the sea to Hispaniola, 161 kilometres (100 miles) distant, to get help. Few of those left behind expected them to survive such a dangerous journey.

As time went on, some rebel Spaniards began to believe Columbus had stranded them deliberately. One day a group of them attacked Columbus and his loyal followers, shouting, 'Kill the Admiral and his men!' In the battle that followed, some of the rebels were killed and the rest were forced to move to another part of the island.

After four days' rowing, Mendez managed to reach Hispaniola and raise the alarm. However, **governor** Ovando was in no hurry to rescue the troublesome Columbus. Eventually, on 28 June 1504, a ship reached Jamaica to take the bedraggled men back to Santo Domingo. When Columbus, tired and sick, stepped ashore two weeks later, Ovando greeted him. Columbus's son Ferdinand described this false show of affection as 'the kiss of a scorpion'.

In Columbus's words:

'Let me only say, my Lord, that my hope has been and is that you will not spare yourself to save me, and I am certain of it, for all my senses inform me.'

(From a letter written by Columbus to Ovando and sent with Mendez)

The coat of arms granted to Christopher Columbus and his descendants. At the top is the castle of Castile and the lion of León in Spain. At the bottom are the islands he discovered and the ships' anchors representing his naval background.

The end of an extraordinary life

A month after being rescued, at the end of July 1504, Columbus and most of his men set sail homewards for Spain. He was now 53 years old and white-haired. He would never return again to the islands that he had first reached twelve years earlier.

A forgotten voice

After a rough crossing, the ship eventually reached the port of Sanlucar de Barrameda, near Seville on 7 November. Columbus was now a very sick man and was convinced that he had only a few more years to live. In his remaining years, he was determined to fight to restore his good name and to win back the fortune he felt he had been cheated out of when replaced as governor.

Columbus's hopes were dashed when Queen Isabella died just nine days after he returned. He wrote letters to Ferdinand, hoping for royal support, but had no response. He was increasingly a forgotten figure as the rush to **colonize** and profit from the 'New World' gathered speed.

DEATH OF QUEEN ISABELLA

On 26 November 1504, Queen Isabella died in the city of Medina del Campo. She was 53 years old, the same age as Columbus. Her body was taken back for burial in her mausoleum in the cathedral of Granada where it rests today. With her death Columbus lost his most loyal and powerful patron.

Final days

For most of the time Columbus was too ill to travel from Seville to meet the king himself. His son Diego was now attached to the **royal court** and handled his father's affairs. Columbus eventually managed to travel to Segovia where he met the king. Ferdinand listened to him politely but Columbus's pleas were ignored. On 20 May 1506, Christopher Columbus died in a Franciscan **monastery** in the city of Valladolid, with his two sons Diego and Ferdinand and his brother Diego by his bed.

Even after his death, however, Christopher Columbus never stopped travelling. His body was first buried in the monastery in Valladolid, but three years later his son Diego had it transferred to a new family tomb in Seville. After Diego's own death, Columbus's bones were taken all the way to Santo Domingo. In 1795, when Hispaniola was captured by the French, the bones were moved to Havana in Cuba. Finally, in 1898, they were returned to Spain and buried in an elaborate tomb in the cathedral of Seville. There they remain to this day.

A sailor stands guard at the magnificent tomb of Christopher Columbus in Seville Cathedral. His body was moved to this final resting place nearly 400 years after his death.

The legacy of Columbus

YOU CAN FOLLOW THE ROUTES OF COLUMBUS'S FOUR EXPEDITIONS ON PAGES 42–3.

Christopher Columbus is famous throughout the world as the explorer who 'discovered' America. However, he died still believing he had reached the **Indies** and that Japan and **Cathay** lay just beyond.

If he had explored the coastlines of Central and South America more during his third and fourth expeditions, Columbus might have realized he had found an entire continent. However, it was another Italian explorer, called Amerigo Vespucci (1451–1512), who first described the continent in a book published in 1507, the year after Columbus's death. It was thus named America after him rather than 'Columbia' after Columbus.

THE VIKINGS IN AMERICA

We now know that Columbus was not the first European to reach the Americas. That was achieved in about 1000, when a party of Vikings led by Leif Ericsson landed on the north-eastern coast of America, where Newfoundland is today. They made a number of settlements but all ended in failure and the route west from Europe was forgotten until Columbus made the journey 500 years later.

Statue of Christopher Columbus at St Anne's Bay, Jamaica. After Columbus first sailed to the area, many more European explorers followed and colonized the Caribbean islands and the mainland of America.

Changing history

No other journey of exploration has led to so much. Columbus's discoveries, and those of the other explorers who came after him, eventually opened the way to the European **colonization** of America. This ultimately created great wealth in Spain and the rest of Europe, but led also to the complete destruction of many ancient ways of life.

Through **persecution** and ignorance, a new culture, religion and language were imposed upon the local people. Today, many Native American people feel very bitter that for centuries their traditional customs and religions were crushed and swept aside. They are now trying to revive many of their old traditions.

Magnificent failure

Columbus boasted and bullied, exaggerated and lied. Most of his expeditions ended in failure and even disaster and he died a broken and bitter man. Even so, his achievement was incredible. His unwavering belief in himself and his missions led him to survive shipwreck, rebellion and disease. He has been described as a magnificent failure, but his failure to find a way to the Indies led to an even greater success: the rediscovery of America for Europe. By achieving this he changed the course of history forever.

> ### In Columbus's words:
>
> *'This is enough. And thus the eternal God, Our Lord, gives to all those who walk in His way triumph over things which appear to be impossible, and this was notably one.'*
>
> (From a letter written by Columbus describing the outcome of his first voyage)

A map of the 'New World' made in 1608 by the Dutch mapmaker Pieter Van Den Keere. It is based upon Columbus's voyage of 1492 and shows many of the islands he discovered.

41

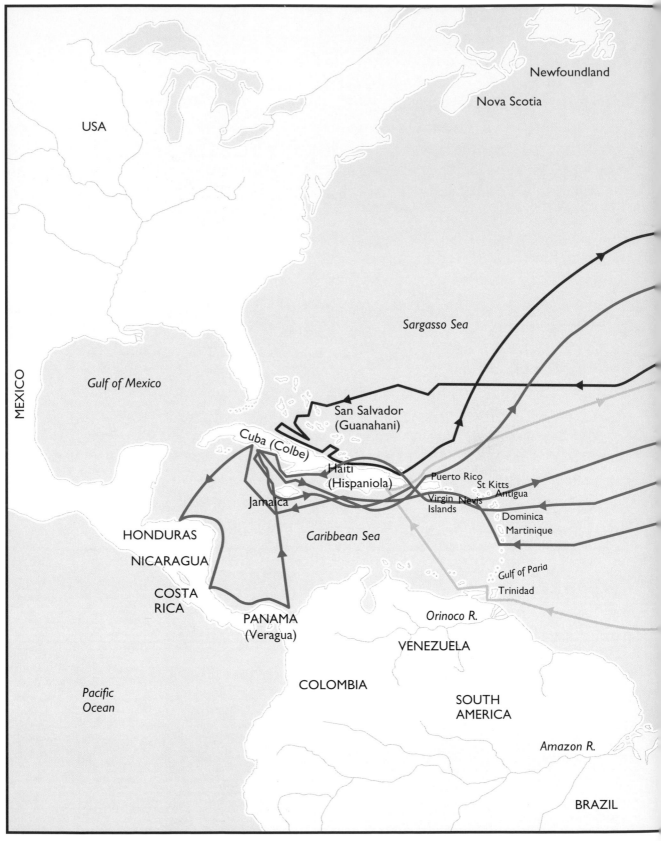

Newfoundland

Nova Scotia

USA

Sargasso Sea

MEXICO

Gulf of Mexico

San Salvador
(Guanahani)

Cuba (Colbe)

Haiti
(Hispaniola)

Puerto Rico
St Kitts
Antigua
Virgin   Nevis
Islands
Dominica
Martinique

Jamaica

Caribbean Sea

HONDURAS

NICARAGUA

Gulf of Paria
Trinidad

COSTA
RICA

PANAMA
(Veragua)

Orinoco R.

VENEZUELA

COLOMBIA

Pacific
Ocean

SOUTH
AMERICA

Amazon R.

BRAZIL

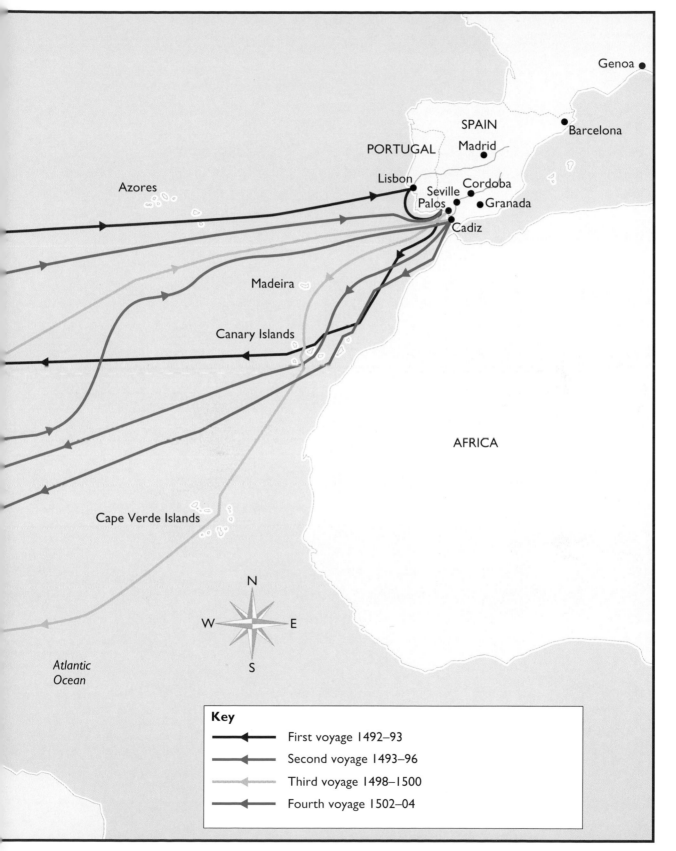

Genoa •

SPAIN

PORTUGAL   Madrid •

Azores

Lisbon •   Seville   Cordoba
            Palos   •   • Granada
                    • Cadiz

Barcelona •

Madeira

Canary Islands

AFRICA

Cape Verde Islands

N
W   E
S

Atlantic
Ocean

Key

First voyage 1492–93

Second voyage 1493–96

Third voyage 1498–1500

Fourth voyage 1502–04

Timeline

1451	Birth of Christopher Columbus in Genoa, Italy.
1453	Turks capture Constantinople, capital city of the Byzantine Empire.
1469	Marriage of King Ferdinand of Aragon and Queen Isabella of Castile.
1476	Columbus moves to Lisbon, Portugal.
c.1480	Marriage of Columbus to Felipa Perestrello e Moniz.
1485	Columbus moves to Spain.
1487	Portugese expedition under Bartolemeu Dias rounds the southern tip of Africa.
1492	Ferdinand and Isabella capture the southern Spanish city of Granada.
	Columbus's first expedition sets sail for the East.
1493	Columbus returns in triumph to Spain.
	Second expedition sets sail.
1494	Battle of Vega Real.
1496	Columbus returns to Spain
1497	John Cabot, sailing from England, reaches the coast of Canada.
1498	Columbus's third expedition sets sail.
	Portuguese expedition under Vasco da Gama reaches the port of Calicut in India.
1500	Columbus arrested and shipped back to Spain.
1502	Nicolás de Ovando appointed new **Governor** of the Indies.
	Columbus sets sail on fourth and final expedition.
1503	He is shipwrecked on Jamaica.
1504	He returns to Spain for the last time.
	Death of Queen Isabella of Spain.
1506	Death of Christopher Columbus.
1507	America is named after Amerigo Vespucci.

Places to visit and further reading

Places to visit

British Museum – Museum of Mankind, London

Museo Naval, Madrid, Spain

Museo de la Torre del Oro, Seville, Spain

National Maritime Museum, Greenwich, London (You can visit the museum
website at www.nmm.ac.uk)

Natural History Museum, Kensington, London

Peabody Museum of Archaeology and Ethnology, Cambridge, USA

Websites

1492 Exhibition:
www.ibiblio.org/expo/1492.exhibit/c-Columbus/columbus.html

Christopher Columbus and the 'New World':
www.geocities.com/columbus_website/index.htm

Discovery:
www.discovery.com

The History Channel:
www.thehistorychannel.co.uk/index

Lake Champlain Maritime Museum, USA:
www.lcmm.org

The Royal Geographical Society:
www.rgs.org

Further reading

Clare, John: *Christopher Columbus* (Bodley Head, 1992)

Hills, Ken: *Christopher Columbus* (Kingfisher, 1990)

McKee, Alexander: *A World Too Vast* (Souvenir Press, 1990)

Sources

Columbus, Ferdinand Fernandez-Armesto (Oxford University Press, 1991)

The Life of Admiral Christopher Columbus, Ferdinand Columbus (Greenwood
Press, 1978)

Glossary

ammunition missiles, such as bullets or rockets, that are shot from a weapon such as a gun or cannon

arthritis inflammation of the joints, creating severe pain and stiffness

astronomy (astronomer) study of the stars and planets

audience chamber official room where a monarch or head of state receives visitors

backing approval and/or money (sponsorship) for a project

brazier metal basket for burning charcoal

cargo goods carried on board a ship

cassava American plant, the root of which is used as food

Cathay old European name for China

city-state independent state made up of a single city and its surrounding territories

colonization act of settling a land with new people

conquer gain control of a place or people

convert change religious beliefs by persuasion, either by choice or by force

crow's-nest lookout platform high up on a ship's mast

doldrums area of the sea along the Equator where there is very little wind

eclipse total or partial covering of the Sun or Moon. A solar eclipse occurs when the Moon passes between the Sun and the Earth; a lunar eclipse when the Earth passes between the Sun and the Moon.

execute put a person to death

flagship most important ship in the fleet, on which the commander of the fleet travels

governor person who governs or rules a province on behalf of a monarch or other head of state

Holy Trinity Christian belief that God exists simultaneously as Himself (Father), Jesus (Son) and as His work on Earth (Holy Spirit)

hull main body of a ship

Indies islands once believed to lie off India, Japan and China

idolator someone who worships 'idols', statues of gods

lookout person on board ship appointed to keep watch against danger

massacre kill brutally in large numbers

merchandise goods bought and sold by merchants and shopkeepers

monastery residence of a religious community of monks

Muslim follower of the religion of Islam

mutiny rebellion by seamen against their senior officers

navigator person in charge of plotting a route and directing a ship along it

Ocean Sea old European name for the Atlantic Ocean

persecution ill-treatment of people because of their culture, religion or appearance

prior head of a religious community

royal court official household of a king or queen

rudder large steering paddle at the stern (back) of a ship

Spice Islands islands in South-east Asia, now known as the Molucca or Maluku Islands of Indonesia, where many spices grew

timbers shaped wooden pieces used to build a ship

vegetation group of different plants growing in a place

Index